C P
CANDLEWICK PRESS

SMART PHONE

MOVIE MAKER

Bryan Michael Stoller
illustrated by Victor Beuren

Text by Bryan Michael Stoller
Illustrations by Victor Beuren

First U.S. edition 2017

Library of Congress Catalog Card Number pending
ISBN 978-0-7636-9411-1

16 17 18 19 20 21 HHO 10 9 8 7 6 5 4 3 2 1

Printed in Shenzhen, Guangdong, China

This book was typeset in Fourth Grader Font and Bodoni Hand.
The illustrations were created digitally.

Candlewick Press
99 Dover Street
Somerville, Massachusetts 02144
visit us at www.candlewick.com

The Quarto Team

Designer: Dan Bramall • Editor: Matthew Morgan
Creative Director: Jonathan Gilbert • Publisher: Zeta Jones

CANDLEWICK PRESS

SMART PHONE MOVIE MAKER

The essential guide for creating epic movies from a small screen.

MAKING MOVIES WITH YOUR SMARTPHONE

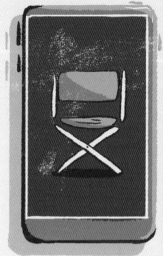

LET'S MAKE MOVIES!

Welcome to the exciting world of making movies! If you own a smartphone (or are allowed to borrow someone else's) then you have a complete movie studio that fits in your pocket. Not only can you shoot your own movie using a smartphone, you can do almost every other phase of movie production, too—from planning your story to casting your film to editing your footage to adding special effects. Everything you need is right there at your fingertips!

PART 1: BEFORE YOU SHOOT

Before you shoot, you'll need to come up with an idea for the story of your movie and then organize your ideas into shots. In this section, you'll discover how to create your own storyboards using the blank storyboard sheets that come with this book. Then you'll need to put your crew together and cast each character from friends, classmates, neighbors, and family. Imagine making your mom and dad stars!

PART 2: LIGHTS, SMARTPHONE, ACTION!

In this section, you'll find great tips on everything from guiding your actors to choosing the right shot for each scene. Save yourself time and trouble by avoiding common shooting mistakes (for example, if you have airplane mode on your phone, turn it on so a phone call doesn't ruin your shoot). Find out how to light each scene, record sound, and even create your own animation!

PART 3: POSTPRODUCTION

After you've shot your movie on your smartphone, it's time to start editing and adding special effects and credits. After that, you'll put together the smartphone projector that comes with this book.

Then you just need to give tickets out to your audience and make some popcorn. It's SHOWTIME!

CHOOSE YOUR STORY IDEA

Do you have a great idea for a movie? Ideas can come from anywhere: from a crazy dream to a conversation you overheard on the bus. Many TV shows and movies are inspired by real-life events, and many moviemakers put their own twist on a news story to create an original idea. Stories are happening all around you, all the time. Keep your eyes and ears open!

THE POWER OF DREAMS

Do you remember your dreams? Keep a notebook (or your smartphone) by your bed and write them down or dictate them as soon as you get up. This way you won't forget a brilliant idea you dream up while you're asleep. If your dreams are vivid, you might come up with the plot of an entire movie!

READ ALL ABOUT IT!

Keep up-to-date with the news. Read magazines, newspapers, books, and Internet articles. A real-life story might trigger a great movie idea. For example, reading about miners being trapped underground might spark a story about your neighbor's dog falling down a well. What happens next is up to you!

WHO, WHAT, WHERE?

Sometimes stories come from the people, places, and things around you. Maybe you live in a spooky old house that would be perfect for a Halloween movie. Or perhaps you think your friends would make great werewolves. Do your friend's parents own an ice-cream shop or work in an office? See if they'll let you film there. (And see if they'll give you free ice cream while you're at it!)

BRAINSTORM YOUR IDEAS

Once you have a basic idea, it's time to develop it into a story with a beginning, a middle, and an end. Sometimes talking to your friends and family about your movie can help you figure out plot problems or come up with new ideas. Maybe your friends will add some ideas of their own, too.

WHICH GENRE?

The tone of your movie will depend on what genre, or type, of movie it is. Will you make a comedy or a thriller? A romance, sci-fi, or horror film, or an action movie? The same basic story will be completely different depending on whether you tell it as a drama or a comedy, for example. So decide on the genre of your movie while you're working on your story idea. Think about which genres you enjoy. Make the kind of film that you like watching!

Hints & Tips

You don't need to write a full screenplay to start making movies. As long as you have a beginning, a middle, and an end, you can start shooting. You can get your actors to improvise the scenes (make them up as they go along).

FROM IDEA TO STORY

How do ideas become stories? First, you have to let your imagination run wild. Keep asking "What if?" What if that sound you heard was a spaceship? What if that dog could talk? What if your friend was really a secret agent? What if your parents' car could fly?

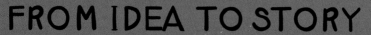

BEGINNINGS AND ENDINGS

Every story has a beginning, a middle, and an end. The beginning of your story should catch your audience's attention and set up the premise—the central idea of the story. Ask yourself, "What does my main character want?" The middle should hold your audience's attention and introduce obstacles that prevent your character from getting what they want. The end should bring your story to a conclusion. Your main character will finally get what they want (if your movie has a happy ending) or not get what they want (if your movie has a sad ending).

Hints & Tips

Write less rather than more. Try to summarize your whole story in one paragraph. Then expand the story to fill a page. Ask yourself: "What does my character want? And why can't they get it?"

INDEX CARDS

To see your story as a whole, write an idea for each scene on a blank index card. Place them on the floor and rearrange them, changing the order of your story. If you are missing any crucial moments in your movie, write them on new index cards and insert them between the other scenes. If you have repeated any moments, or if your movie feels too long, you can take index cards away.

WRITE A SCREENPLAY

A screenplay is a written version of your script that contains the characters' dialogue (the words they speak) as well as their movements, actions, and facial expressions. Online apps will automatically set your story into a standard screenplay format that all professional Hollywood writers use. When you print your screenplay, it will look like a real movie script! You can also create a PDF of your script and send it to your cast and crew.

A HOLLYWOOD SCREENPLAY

This is what a professionally formatted Hollywood screenplay looks like:

SCENE NUMBER: Numbering scenes is useful when you are organizing your shooting schedule. Everyone will immediately know which scenes you're shooting on which day.

PARENTHETICALS: Words in brackets express emotions or how a line is delivered by the actor.

PAGE NUMBER: So you can tell if a page of your script is missing!

CHARACTER NAMES: These are always in capital letters when a character is speaking.

SCENE ACTION: This describes the action you see taking place. Make sure you don't include things an audience won't be able to see, like a character's thoughts.

DIALOGUE: These are the words your characters say.

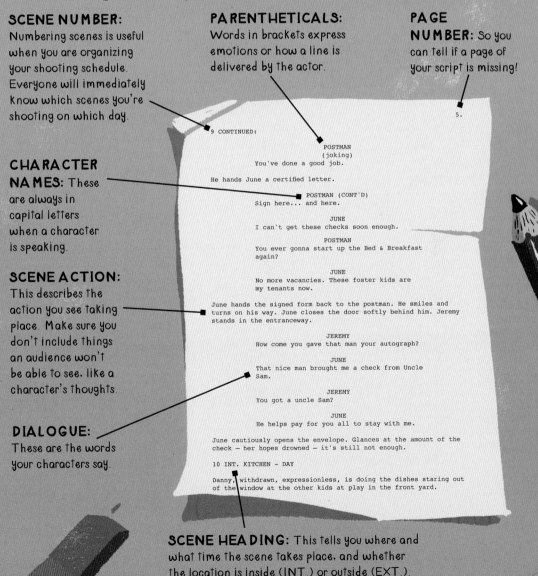

```
9 CONTINUED:

                         POSTMAN
                        (joking)
              You've done a good job.

He hands June a certified letter.

                         POSTMAN (CONT'D)
              Sign here... and here.

                         JUNE
              I can't get these checks soon enough.

                         POSTMAN
              You ever gonna start up the Bed & Breakfast
              again?

                         JUNE
              No more vacancies. These foster kids are
              my tenants now.

June hands the signed form back to the postman. He smiles and
turns on his way. June closes the door softly behind him. Jeremy
stands in the entranceway.

                         JEREMY
              How come you gave that man your autograph?

                         JUNE
              That nice man brought me a check from Uncle
              Sam.

                         JEREMY
              You got a uncle Sam?

                         JUNE
              He helps pay for you all to stay with me.

June cautiously opens the envelope. Glances at the amount of the
check — her hopes drowned — it's still not enough.

10 INT. KITCHEN - DAY

Danny, withdrawn, expressionless, is doing the dishes staring out
of the window at the other kids at play in the front yard.
```

SCENE HEADING: This tells you where and what time the scene takes place, and whether the location is inside (INT.) or outside (EXT.).

9

SHOT BY SHOT

It's nearly time to shoot your movie. But where will you position your camera for each shot? Work this out before you start filming by making a shot list. A "shot" is what you film from the moment you turn a camera on to the moment you turn it off. Each scene in your movie will be divided into shots, and each shot will be different depending on what you want to show and what you want your audience to feel. For instance, you might have a wide shot of a farm burning down followed by a close-up of the farmer crying.

1. Danny sits on park bench. Camera moves in closer.

2. Close-up of coins in his hands.

3. Shot of water fountain wishing well. Camera pulls out to reveal Danny standing at the well.

4. Shot of water flowing into the well as several coins plop into the water.

5. Close-up of Danny's face, eyes closed, thinking of his wish.

MAKE A SHOT LIST

A shot list looks very similar to a shopping or to-do list. Give each shot in your film a number and write down in detail what the camera will see in each shot of your movie. You can make a shot list using a memo or list app on your smartphone.

CREATE A STORYBOARD

If you want to see what your movie will look like before you shoot it, create a storyboard. Storyboards turn your words into pictures and help you organize your shots so that you can figure out what's required for each one: how many actors, the type of shot, and if you'll need special effects.

Study some of your favorite comic books and look at the different angles the illustrators use in each panel. Angles in comics are often exaggerated, which could work for your movie, too. You might want to color in your storyboards to help show the mood you want for each particular scene.

HOW A STORYBOARD WORKS

Each panel in your storyboard represents one shot in your movie.

Number each panel so you know which shot it represents.

Leave room beneath each panel to write a description of the shot.

1 ....

2 ....

3 ....

4 ....

5 ....

6 ....

Write down any dialogue and technical notes about lighting or sound.

Draw arrows to show which direction your actors will move.

Arrows can also show the way a camera will move within a shot.

SPECIAL SHOTS ONLY

If you don't want to storyboard your entire film, that's OK. You might just want to storyboard really complicated shots that use special effects or elaborate camera moves to make sure everyone on your crew is clear about how those shots will work.

MAKE YOUR OWN STORYBOARD

If you're an artist, you can color in each panel so your storyboard is a work of art in its own right. But if you don't like drawing, you can still create your own storyboard. Here are a few easy ways to create the pictures in your storyboard panels.

STICK FIGURES

Use the blank storyboard sheets included with this book to draw your own storyboards. Even simple stick figures can give a sense of what's happening as the story develops. You could use different-colored pens to represent different characters or give them a defining characteristic like a hat or hairstyle.

1 ....

2 ....

STORYBOARD APPS

You'll find lots of free apps to help you draw storyboards on your smartphone—from simple drawing apps to those designed specifically for making storyboards. Many storyboard apps come with libraries of characters, props, and locations that you can easily drag and drop into your storyboard panels.

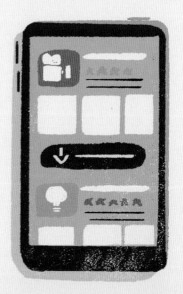

PHOTO SHOOTS

What if you don't have the patience for drawing? Pull out your smartphone and start taking photos. Ask your actors to pose for each panel in your storyboard. Take the photo from the position the camera will be in when you shoot your movie. If it's an over-the-shoulder shot of one of your actors looking at another, take the photo over the shoulder of your actor. Put these photos in your storyboard app or stick them to a piece of paper and add dialogue and a description to each panel.

TOYS AND MODELS

You don't need actors to take photos for your storyboard. You can use everyday things like salt and pepper shakers, toy cars, dolls, or cutlery to represent the characters in your story. Get them into position and take photos of them with your smartphone!

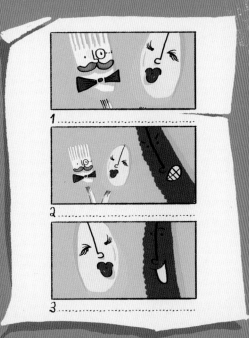

THE FINISHED PRODUCT

When your storyboard is ready, email copies to your cast and crew or print them and give them out before you start shooting. Your storyboard will bring your movie to life and ensure that everyone shares your vision. It's a good idea to display a copy on a wall of your set to remind everyone what's going to happen in each shot.

CREW MEMBERS: ASSEMBLE!

You don't need a big Hollywood crew to make a movie with your smartphone. You can operate the camera and shoot it yourself. If you're acting in your movie as well, you can take turns with your other actors to shoot the scenes.

MEET THE CREW

You can recruit your movie crew from your family, friends, and classmates—anyone who likes to be creative and have fun. Different people in a crew need different strengths, so there will be something for everyone to do!

* The DIRECTOR oversees all the creative aspects of a movie.
* The PRODUCER looks after the non-creative aspects of the movie, such as raising money, hiring the crew, and finding an audience.
* The DIRECTOR OF PHOTOGRAPHY is the chief of the camera and lighting crew. He or she works with the director to decide on the camera's movements. On lower-budget productions, this person often works as the camera operator.
* The PRODUCTION SOUND MIXER ensures the sound is clear and mixed at the right levels so that dialogue and sound effects aren't too loud or too quiet.
* The PRODUCTION DESIGNER is responsible for how a movie looks. On a smartphone production, the producer and/or director can perform this role.

* Working with the production designer is a PROPS MASTER, who looks after props, and a COSTUME DESIGNER, who decides what the actors should wear.
* The FILM EDITOR puts the movie together in postproduction, choosing shots alongside the director.

A STAR IS BORN!

Almost everyone wants to be a movie star, and you can give your friends the big break they've been waiting for! You can write parts especially for particular people, but most of the time you'll want your actors to audition to ensure you give the right parts to the right people.

AUDITIONS

If your film has dialogue, create some "sides" (pages from your script) and give them to your actors before the audition so they can practice. In the audition, ask each actor to read out the sides with you or another actor. Choose a particularly emotional scene, or a scene where the character has a lot of dialogue, so you can really test your performers. Don't be afraid to direct your actors during the audition — this will show whether you'll work well together and whether your actors are good at following instructions!

CAUGHT ON FILM

Film your auditions so that you can look back over them later. Show them to your friends to see who they think is best for each part. Ask your actors to "slate" before they start auditioning on camera. Slating is when the actor states their name and contact information. This way you won't have to remember who is who and how to contact them.

15

COSTUMES, PROPS, AND LOCATIONS

Costumes, props, and locations can have a huge effect on the mood of a movie and can also be lots of fun to arrange. It's worth spending time assembling all the things you need beforehand, so that you're not running around on the day of filming, which can hold up your schedule and be frustrating for your cast and crew.

COSTUMES

Costumes are the clothes an actor wears when in character. They can be bought or, if you or someone you know is good at designing and sewing, made from scratch. Costumes range from everyday clothes like T-shirts and jeans to a police uniform or an alien monster's outfit. If there's a special costume you need and you can't make it, ask your friends. It's surprising what people have in their closets.

PROPS

A prop is any object that your actors use during filming. It could be the cup they drink from or the chair they sit on. If your actor eats anything during a shot, then this is considered a prop, too. Always go through your shot list and prepare what you will need in advance of filming. And make sure your cast and crew don't eat all the props before you get the shot!

CONTINUITY

Continuity means ensuring that your actor wears the same clothes and carries the same props from scene to scene. If your actor is leaving the house wearing a cowboy hat and carrying a cell phone, for example, make sure he is wearing the cowboy hat and carrying the phone when he arrives at his destination.

Take photos of your actors every time you shoot a scene. This will help you remember what your actors are wearing so you can make sure they look the same in any scenes that follow on. Make sure you match their clothes, jewelry, hats, shoes, and props—and their hairstyles and makeup, too.

LOCATION, LOCATION

A movie location is the place where you shoot your film. The right location can have a huge impact on the atmosphere of a film. If you film everything in a tiny closet, for instance, your film will feel very tense. Look around your house or neighborhood to see if there are any good places to shoot. Always ask for permission from the person who owns the property before you start filming, and never put yourself in danger just to get a good shot!

Hints & Tips

Avoid using T-shirts with logos and brand names on them. They're distracting, and why advertise a product unless they give you money or free stuff? Avoid clothes with stripes, as these can get distorted on camera and look as though they're wiggling around!

THE RIGHT DIRECTION

It's time to direct your movie! Directing involves everything from guiding your actors to deciding how the camera should move and selecting the right shots to capture the action.

REHEARSING

Take time to rehearse dialogue with your actors so that they sound natural — as though they're having a real conversation rather than reading out words written on a page. If the words don't sound natural, let your actor change the dialogue slightly (without changing the meaning of the words) so that they feel more comfortable saying them. Give your actors feedback: Do you want them to say a line more angrily or happily? Do you want them to move in a certain way? Make sure you encourage them and tell them when they've done something really well, too.

BLOCKING YOUR SCENES

Blocking your scenes means working out where your actors move in relation to the camera. Will they just stand still and have a conversation? Or will they do things during the shot like make dinner, have a sword fight, or go for a walk? It's important to practice this so you know what the camera will capture during each shot. Remember that the position of the camera and what it is focused on tells the audience what's important in a scene.

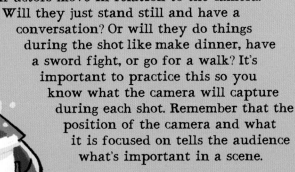

FIGHT SCENES

If there's a fight scene in your movie, make sure you rehearse and block this really carefully before you shoot so that no one gets hurt. A fight scene is like a dance. Every swing, punch, and roll is planned beforehand and timed perfectly to make it look real. Your actors will never actually touch each other during the fight, but the camera angle you use will make the punches look real. You can add the sound of a punch in post-production to make the scene even more realistic.

Hints & Tips

It's up to you as the director to speed up or slow down the performance of the scenes and to change things that aren't working. Most importantly, make sure your cast and crew are comfortable and having a great time!

A MOVING PICTURE

Don't keep your smartphone camera still for every shot. Moving your camera can create real emotional impact and drama. After all, a movie is called a motion picture, not a still picture! The advantage of shooting on your smartphone is that it's light and easy to move around, so you can follow your actors and move closer and farther away from them to make your shots more interesting.

SHOOT!

You're ready to shoot your movie! First, decide which kind of shot you'll use. You have three main choices: the wide or "establishing" shot, the medium shot, and the close-up.

WIDE SHOT

This shot sets the scene by revealing where the main characters are before the camera starts to move in closer. This orientates your audience so they know the setting and don't feel lost. A wide shot can show a building, a beach, a street, or even a moving aircraft.

Hints & Tips

A wide shot of a planet might set the scene for a film based on a different world. Hang a ball on a thin nylon string and suspend it in front of a piece of paper that's painted to look like space. Move your camera slowly in a C shape around your planet. In postproduction you can add special effects to make the planet seem more alien.

MEDIUM SHOT

A medium shot is wide enough to show one to three people, usually from the waist up. The basic rule is that the shot should comfortably frame the characters in the scene.

CLOSE-UP

A close-up usually shows a single actor's face (unless a couple is locked in an embrace). This kind of shot emphasizes a character's emotions.

EXTREME CLOSE-UP

If you zoom in even closer on an actor's face — or even just show their eyes — this is an extreme close-up. This shot should be used for capturing really intense emotional moments — when your character is feeling extremely sad, happy, or angry and you want the audience to connect with them.

SHOOT FROM ABOVE

Film your actor from above to make the character appear small, powerless, or weak. This shot is useful if you want to show that a character feels scared or vulnerable.

SHOOT FROM BELOW

Position your camera low on the ground and point it upward to film your actor. This will make the character look bigger, stronger, or more menacing, as if they're towering over the audience.

YOUR GENRE

Different genres of film tell different kinds of stories. Each genre also has a distinct look and feel. Watch as many movies as you can in different genres and study the cinematic tricks that directors use. How are the shots framed? Is the movie fast-paced or slow? What's the lighting like? What kinds of colors are used?

HORROR

If you're shooting a scene where a monster is stomping toward you, point your smartphone upward toward it. Light the monster from behind so that it's in shadow. Lift one end of your smartphone so the shot is slightly crooked — this will make the shot feel even creepier.

DETECTIVE MOVIE/FILM NOIR

Detective movies (also called film noir) use lots of shadows and muted colors. Sometimes they're filmed entirely in black and white. You can use an app or edit the colors in postproduction to make them less bright. This genre often features a voice-over from the main character, narrating the action.

COMEDY

Comedies are usually fast paced. The characters talk quickly and the action is snappy. Colors are usually bright and cheerful. Encourage your actors to speed up their dialogue and exaggerate their action, and make sure you edit the movie tightly so there aren't any long pauses. Remember, comedy is about surprise — don't let your audience guess what's going to happen next!

ACTION

Action movies feature fast, adrenaline-fueled chase or fight sequences, often filmed with shaky shots (see below) to create a sense of excitement and mayhem. Cut quickly between short shots—if you're showing a chase, you might have a shot of feet running followed by a close-up of a sweating face, then a shot of another person catching up.

SHAKY CAMERA

Many smartphones come with a steady mode for those who can't quite keep the camera steady for a smooth shot. If you're going to emphasize the excitement in your action or war film, turn steady mode off. Otherwise your smartphone will correct your intentionally shaky shots.

SCIENCE FICTION

If you're shooting a sci-fi movie, you'll have to get creative. Try making your own costumes and props. You could use puppets as monsters or green face paint to make your actors look like aliens, or fill your set with tiny furniture to make someone look like a giant. And what about a homemade UFO on a piece of string? Keep your lighting low and mysterious for shots filmed on other planets and add effects in postproduction.

GREAT GADGETS

The great thing about shooting movies on your smartphone is that your camera barely weighs more than a deck of playing cards, so you don't need heavy equipment. You can make or buy miniature versions of the accessories and gadgets that professional filmmakers use. These include tripods (stands that hold your camera still), cranes (devices that lift your camera in the air so you can shoot from high above the ground or from unusual angles), and dollies (wheeled platforms that keep the camera steady during moving shots).

MAKE YOUR OWN TRIPOD

For no cost at all, you can make a stand for your smartphone out of a plastic or polystyrene cup.

1. Using scissors, cut two wide slits on each side of the cup.

2. Trim about 3/4 of an inch (2 cm) from the top of the cup to make it shorter.

3. Your stand is ready! Slide your smartphone into the slits.

4. Use masking tape to secure the smartphone to the cup so that you can move the camera as you shoot.

UNUSUAL SHOTS

Flexible smartphone tripods (also known as octopus stands) are inexpensive and great for shooting from tricky places. The bendy legs can be wrapped around poles, lamps, or even bike handlebars, so you can capture shots from almost any angle.

FILMING WITH A SELFIE STICK

You don't need a studio movie crane to capture low-to-the-ground or overhead shots; an inexpensive, lightweight selfie stick will do the trick.

GROUND SHOTS

Follow objects close to the ground by holding the selfie stick upside down. You can use it to track the movement of a remote-controlled car, a robot, a toy train on a track, or a dog walking along the street.

HIGHER SHOTS

A selfie stick also works well as a movie crane for higher shots. Attach your smartphone to the selfie stick and hold it high in the air. You could shoot a crowd of people from above, film over a wall or fence, or film something out of your reach, like a birdhouse in a tree.

SKATEBOARD DOLLY

A skateboard is all you need to capture smooth moving shots low to the ground. Mount your smartphone on your tripod. Then place the tripod on a skateboard and push it gently along the ground as you film. Don't let go of your skateboard, though, or your smartphone might fall off and break! Alternatively, you can sit on the skateboard holding your smartphone as a friend pushes you.

TECHNICAL TIPS

Follow these technical tips to make sure your movie looks
and sounds as professional as possible.

FILM IN LANDSCAPE

A common mistake that many people make when they start
making films on their smartphones is to hold the device in
portrait position (upright) during filming. TV, YouTube, Vimeo,
and cinema screens are landscape (wider than they are tall), so
to make sure your image fills the whole screen, turn the phone
sideways and film in the landscape setting. This is also called
widescreen. If you shoot
in portrait mode, there
will be a black bar on
each side of your movie
when you view it.

SOUND

If you have bad audio that is tinny or unclear,
it will be harder for the audience to enjoy your
movie. If possible, use a separate microphone
when you're filming rather than your
smartphone's built-in microphone. The built-in
microphone will work well for close-ups, but
once your actors are farther away, background
noise will start to interfere with their dialogue.

DIRECTIONAL MIC

A directional mic only picks up the sounds right in front of it, so background noise won't get in the way. Point your mic at an actor's face to record their dialogue. For wider shots, attach the mic to a long stick or "boom." Just make sure the mic doesn't get in the shot!

OMNI-DIRECTIONAL MIC

An omni-directional microphone captures audio from all around. Omni-directional microphones are good for recording ambient background sounds, like the sounds of a park or restaurant or the noise of an air conditioner.

LOOPING

If your location is really noisy, like a building site or busy road, you may need to ask your actors to re-record their dialogue after filming is over. This is called looping. When you are editing the film, ask your actors to watch the scene a few times, repeating the dialogue at the same pace as their original performance. When the actors are ready, re-record their dialogue and then insert this into the movie along with separate background sound.

KNOW YOUR LIGHTING

Without proper lighting, your movie will look grainy and unprofessional. The good news is that you can use household lamps with ordinary lightbulbs for indoor shots. Plus, most smartphones don't need much light; the camera automatically brightens things that are too dark and tones down scenes that are too bright.

TYPES OF LIGHT

You'll need at least three lights: a key light, which lights your actor or subject; a balance light, which is positioned opposite the key light and fills in some of the shadows created by the key light; and a backlight, which is positioned behind your actor, out of shot, lighting your actor from behind and making your shot look more three-dimensional.

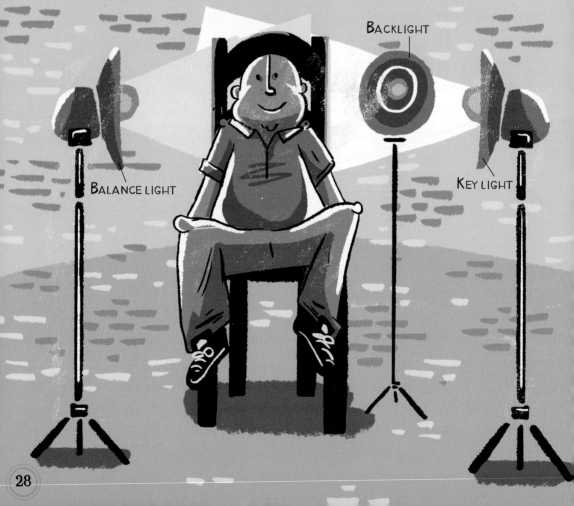

BACKLIGHT

BALANCE LIGHT

KEY LIGHT

DAYLIGHT

The advantage of shooting
outside during the day is that the
sun becomes your movie light:
a pretty big one at that! But if
the sun is shining directly
onto your actors, they
might look washed out on
camera. A good trick is to
bounce the sunlight off a
piece of white cardboard
and reflect a much softer
light onto your actor.

LOW LIGHT

If you're shooting in a location
where there isn't much light,
like a tent, and you just want to
illuminate the faces of your actors,
use a flashlight or the flashlight
app on a friend's smartphone to
shine light on your actors' faces.

SMARTPHONE FLASH

Most smartphones have their own
movie light built in—the flash!
The flash might come in handy if
you're shooting in the dark and you
forget to bring extra lights.

ANIMATION

What if you want talking animals in your movie, but your cat isn't a great actor? If you like drawing, you could animate your movie instead of shooting live actors. Animation is the art of bringing objects or drawings to life. Your favorite cartoons are animated. Some are drawn by hand and some are created digitally.

HOW ANIMATION WORKS

An animation sequence consists of a series of still pictures of a subject (a boy in a cat costume, for instance). Each picture is slightly different. When you watch these pictures one after the other in quick succession, your eyes are tricked into thinking the subject is moving. When you watch cartoons, you're actually seeing 24 separate still pictures (or frames) per second.

CARTOON ANIMATION

Cartoons are easy to create. You don't need any special apps. You just need to shoot one frame at a time on your smartphone. You can do black-and-white drawings on paper, or color them in. Each drawing must be progressive, meaning that the movement must advance slightly in each one. When you see the pictures quickly, one after the other, it will seem as though there is one moving image.

STOP-MOTION

If you want to animate a physical object, like a clay model, you can use stop-motion animation. Take a photo of your model, move or change its shape slightly, and take another photo. You can even use this technique to animate household items like cups and saucers.

CUT-OUTS

Cut-out characters are easy to make and animate. Draw a cartoon character on cardboard, making sure you leave a space between each part of its body. Cut out each body part separately. Hinge the parts together with paper fasteners so that you can bend the character at the joints. Take a picture of your character, move the joints, and take another picture, and so on.

PIXILATION

You can even make an animation using photographs. This is called pixilation. Take photos of your friends, asking them to move slightly between each shot. For instance, ask your friend to sit on the ground and to shift sideways slightly between each photograph. In your final animation, it will seem as though your friend is sliding across the floor.

ANIMATION TIPS AND TRICKS

Here are some techniques to make your animation look as professional as possible.

ANIMATION CYCLES

An easy way to animate a character doing a repetitive action such as running, skipping, or walking is to create an animation cycle. Animation cycles work by using the same drawing or frames over and over again. Just draw your character doing each different stage of the action once and then repeat the cycle of images. You can make your character skip forever using just a few drawings! Animation cycles are used often in cartoons.

TIME-LAPSE ANIMATION

Most smartphones have a time-lapse option, usually in the phone's photo/video app. There are also free time-lapse apps available. Time-lapse lets you control how often your phone takes a photograph. If you wanted to show clouds in the sky zipping by quickly, you might set your smartphone to take one frame every five minutes. The end result would be an animation of the clouds whizzing through the sky as if they are wisps of smoke.

If you set up your smartphone on a tripod and shoot one frame every ten seconds, you can show a person mowing an entire lawn in about one minute.

STOPPING AND STARTING

When you're animating something stopping and starting, remember that it takes time for things to speed up and slow down. To make your animation look realistic, make sure your moving object picks up speed gradually and slows down gradually. Also, when things start moving in real life, they move backward slightly before they start going forward. And when things stop, they keep moving forward for a few frames before they come to a complete standstill.

START

STOP

LOCK DOWN YOUR SMARTPHONE

Remember that with any form of animation, you have to lock down your smartphone while taking individual still photographs. In other words, you must place it on a tripod or solid surface so it doesn't move while you're taking photographs. Be careful that you don't accidentally move your camera when you press the button to snap each frame. There are apps that enable you to take pictures by saying the word "click" instead of touching your phone.

CLICK!

EDIT YOUR MASTERPIECE

Everything you do after you've finished shooting your movie—from editing your film to adding sound effects and any special effects—is called post-production. Editing means organizing all your shots and putting your movie together, which you can do using editing software on your smartphone or on a computer. You'll be able to put all of your shots in the right order, trim them down so they're not too long, and make sure you're telling the best version of your story.

CORRECT THE COLOR

Change the look and mood of your scenes with color filters. Free or inexpensive apps let you play with the colors. Most smartphones have color filters in the still photo settings, and may have color filters for your movies, too.

Hints & Tips

Upload your footage directly from your smartphone to YouTube and edit it in YouTube for no cost! There's even a section on YouTube where you can add transitions, color correction, titles, and copyright-free music.

The original shot below has poor lighting and low contrast between areas of light and dark. The color filter brightens up the image and increases the contrast. If you want to make your shot more dramatic, use a black-and-white filter or apply a color tint such as sepia or blue.

Original shot

Color filter

Black-and-white filter

Sepia filter

ADD MUSIC

Bear in mind that popular music is copyrighted, so you won't be able to use it. The people who own the copyright will charge you lots of money if you do! There are lots of free music apps that will give you access to public-domain music—meaning music that's **FREE** to use. Alternatively, if you play an instrument or if you have friends in the school orchestra or in a band, you can record your own music using a recording app on your smartphone (you'll be able to find a free app to use). E-mail the audio file to yourself and drop it into your movie using your editing software.

SOUND EFFECTS

Sound effects will enhance your movie, making it more emotional or dramatic. Your smartphone is portable, so you can capture audio from real places, like a zoo, a restaurant, or a football game. Because you'll be recording audio from all around you, the microphone built into your smartphone should work well.

You can record an elephant's trumpet with your smartphone and drop it into your movie during postproduction.

ADD SPECIAL EFFECTS

Special effects create the illusion that something extraordinary or magical is happening. There are two main methods for creating special effects. You can generate them while you are shooting—for example, you can simulate an earthquake by shaking your camera and throwing sand or stones into the shot. Alternatively, you can add effects during postproduction using the editing software available on most home computers.

MAKE A GIANT

Forced perspective is an effect you can create by simple framing. Ask an actor to stand close to the camera (in the foreground) and position a second actor in the background. The positioning of the two actors will make the foreground actor look like a giant and make the actor in the background appear tiny.

Ask the actor in the background to react as if he or she is in the palm of a giant. The power of the illusion is partly in the performance!

REVERSE-MOTION EFFECTS

You can create fun reverse-motion effects during editing by clicking the reverse button in your editing software. For example, you could take footage of a girl drinking milk through a straw and reverse it so that she fills the glass with milk from her mouth.

GREEN SCREEN

Shoot your actors in front of a green background, such as green curtains, green poster board, or a green wall. Using editing software, you can replace the green background with footage of any other scene. You can place your actor in any location you like—a football stadium, a desert, or even outer space!

Making Rain

Creating weather special effects is really tricky, so avoid them if you can. If you want to shoot a scene indoors but show that it's raining outside, you can ask a friend to stand outside and spray the window with a garden hose so that water falls on the window, imitating rain.

Make sure your actors aren't wearing any items of green clothing, or green make-up. Otherwise, when you're erasing the green color from the background, your actor will start to disappear, too!

Hints & Tips

The reverse effect works best when there's a good reason for using it. For example, does your film have a character who can turn back time?

Use a basic editing program to erase the green background. Afterward, insert footage of a football stadium, desert, or moonscape to fill the background. This is called layering or compositing. It will look as though your actors are in the new location.

ROLL CREDITS

That's a wrap. You've done it! You have a finished movie. All you need to do is to add the credits—the part at the end of your movie where you list your cast and crew and thank everyone who helped you make your film by lending you things or letting you film on their property. Everybody gets excited when they see their name in the credits of a movie!

TIPS FOR YOUR TITLE

Get creative and reflect the theme of your movie in your credit sequence.

If your film is set at school or at a café, you could use a chalkboard app to give you a black chalkboard background. Choose a pale color for your credits, so that they look as if they're scribbled in chalk.

Produced by YOU
Directed by YOU
Acted by YOU

If your film is set on a boat or near the sea, print your title on paper and place a glass dish filled with water over it. Move the water so that it ripples and shoot your title from above.

If your film is about a painter, you could film someone spraying the title of your movie onto a sheet of paper.

GET THE ORDER RIGHT

This is the order in which credits traditionally appear at the end of Hollywood movies. You might not have people doing all of these different jobs—or you might have even more people to thank! Remember to thank people who weren't in your cast or crew but who helped you out in a "special thanks" section at the end.

CAST (in the order in which they appeared in your movie, or in order of importance)
DIRECTOR
WRITER
PRODUCER
DIRECTOR OF PHOTOGRAPHY
EDITOR
PRODUCTION DESIGNER
COSTUME DESIGNER
PROPS MASTER
CAMERA OPERATOR
PRODUCTION SOUND MIXER

IT'S SHOWTIME!

You've done the hard work. Now it's time to premiere your movie. Dress in your best clothes, imagine you're walking the red carpet, and bask in the praise of your friends and family. The projector that comes with this book is easy to assemble. You can impress your friends by telling them that not only did you make a movie with your smartphone, you constructed the projector, too! Turn to pages 42–44 to learn how to put it together.

INSIDE OR OUT

Point your projector at a white wall inside your house, or project your movie onto a white sheet to premiere your movie in your yard — as long as it's a dark night! Your friends can sit on blankets and eat popcorn while enjoying your masterpiece on the big screen.

ADMIT ONE

Movie tickets to give out to your friends and family are included with this book. Just cut them out and hand them out before your premiere! If you've spent money on making your movie, you might even be able to make some of it back by selling tickets for the performance.

THEMED SHOW

If your movie has a particular theme or genre, like a horror or western, why not encourage the audience to join in by dressing up as zombies or cowboys for the show?

PREPARE YOUR POPCORN

You can buy ready-made bags of popcorn, or you can make microwave, hot-air, or oven-top popcorn. Make sure you ask an adult to help you make it, especially if you use an oven or a hot-air popper. Then serve it in the popcorn box included with this book. Photocopy the popcorn cut-out to create more boxes.

BUILD YOUR PROJECTOR

Now it's time to build your projector! Make sure you construct and try it out before your audience arrives for the screening. You'll need to give yourself plenty of time to make adjustments depending on the space where you're showing your movie.

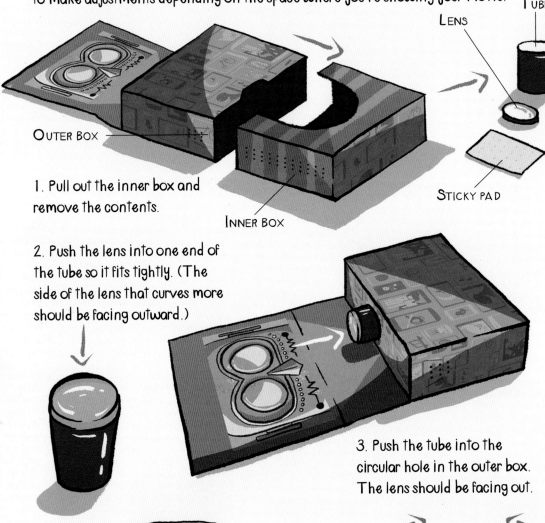

TUBE

LENS

OUTER BOX

INNER BOX

STICKY PAD

1. Pull out the inner box and remove the contents.

2. Push the lens into one end of the tube so it fits tightly. (The side of the lens that curves more should be facing outward.)

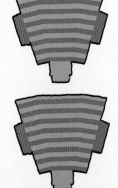

3. Push the tube into the circular hole in the outer box. The lens should be facing out.

4. Press out the two card speakers from the model sheets.

5. Fold the three sides of each speaker inward along the creases to create tabs.

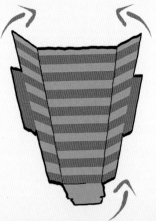

6. Insert the speaker tabs into the slots on either side of the outer box.

7. Fold back the speaker tabs inside the box and tape them flat to the inside.

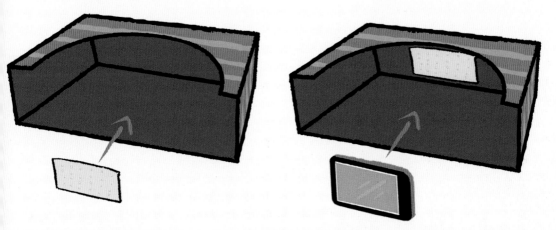

8. Attach the sticky pad to the inside of the inner box.

9. Place your smartphone against the sticky pad, resting its bottom edge on the floor of the box. Push your smartphone against the pad to secure it. (Your phone won't get marked by the sticky pad.)

10. The movie image on your smartphone will need to be playing "upside down" so that the projected image appears correctly on the screen. To fix the orientation, start playing your movie, then swipe up (twice) from the bottom of the screen to bring up your notification bar/control center and press Portrait Orientation Lock: On.

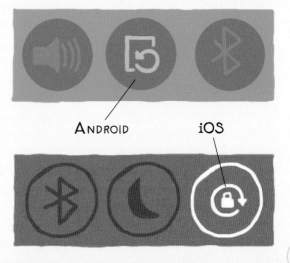

ANDROID   iOS

11. Slide the inner box back into the outer box.

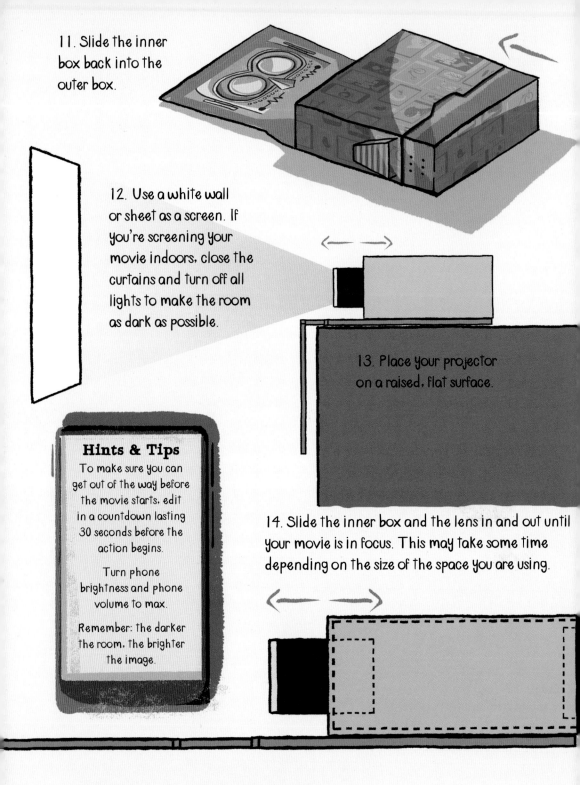

12. Use a white wall or sheet as a screen. If you're screening your movie indoors, close the curtains and turn off all lights to make the room as dark as possible.

13. Place your projector on a raised, flat surface.

Hints & Tips

To make sure you can get out of the way before the movie starts, edit in a countdown lasting 30 seconds before the action begins.

Turn phone brightness and phone volume to max.

Remember: the darker the room, the brighter the image.

14. Slide the inner box and the lens in and out until your movie is in focus. This may take some time depending on the size of the space you are using.

15. Ask your audience to take their seats, turn your smartphone on, and start playing your movie!

MAKE YOUR POPCORN BOX

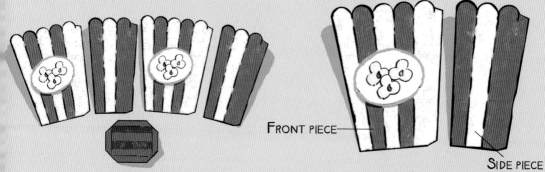

FRONT PIECE

SIDE PIECE

1. Press out the popcorn box pieces. Fold tabs along dotted lines.

2. Run a line of food-safe glue or tape down the tab of your front piece. Press the edge of one of the side pieces to the tab. Do the same with your back piece.

3. You will now have two sections. Join them together by sticking the edge of your front piece to the tab on the side piece of the other section.

4. Take the bottom of your popcorn box and stick one of the long tabs to the bottom edge of your front piece. Go around the box, sticking each tab in turn.

5. Stick the remaining long edge to the side tab to complete your box.

6. Fill the box with popcorn and enjoy!

GLOSSARY

action: a movie that involves fight scenes, violence, and chase scenes

animation: the art of bringing objects or drawings to life, one frame at a time

app: a computer program designed to run on a smartphone

blocking: working out where actors move in relation to the camera

cast: the actors who appear in a movie

continuity: ensuring that actors wear the same clothes and carry the same props from scene to scene

close-up shot: a shot that shows a single actor's face

comedy: a movie designed to make the audience laugh

costume: clothing that actors wear in a movie

costume designer: the person who decides what each actor should wear

crane: a stand that lifts a camera into the air

credits: the list of cast and crew at the beginning and end of a movie

crew: the group of people who help to make a movie

dolly: a camera platform on wheels used for smooth moving shots

film noir: a detective movie

dialogue: the words spoken by a movie's characters

directional microphone: a mic that only picks up sound that it is directly in front of it

director: the person who oversees all the creative aspects of a movie

director of photography: the chief of the camera and lighting crew

editing: organizing the shots and putting a movie together

extreme close-up: a very close-up shot (e.g., showing an actor's eyes)

film editor: the person who puts the movie together in postproduction

genre: the type of movie, such as horror or sci-fi

horror: a movie that aims to scare the audience

location: the place or places where a film is shot

looping: when actors re-record dialogue after filming is over

medium shot: a shot that is wide enough to show one to three people

omni-directional microphone: a microphone that captures audio from all around

pixilation: a type of animation using still photographs

postproduction: all the work done to complete a movie after shooting is finished

premise: the central idea of a story

producer: the person who handles the "non-creative" aspects of a movie

production designer: the person who takes responsibility for how a movie looks

production sound mixer: the person who makes sure the audio is clear

prop: any object that actors use during filming

rehearsal: practicing dialogue and movement before shooting a movie

science fiction/sci-fi: a movie that imagines alternative realities involving imaginary science and technology or aliens

screenplay: a written version of a script

shot: what is filmed from the moment a camera is turned on to the moment it is turned off

shot list: a list of all the shots in a movie

slate: when the actor states their name and contact information on film before an audition

smartphone: a phone with its own camera and ability to download apps

stop-motion: an animation technique using a physical object such as a toy

storyboard: a way of organizing a movie using panels of images

time-lapse: a technique that takes a series of photos over an extended period of time

tripod: a stand that holds a camera still

wide shot: a shot that establishes the location

INDEX